Judy Garland Is Not a Sunrise

poems by

E.F. Schraeder

Finishing Line Press
Georgetown, Kentucky

Judy Garland
Is Not a Sunrise

Copyright © 2023 by E.F. Schraeder
ISBN 979-8-88838-133-5 First Edition
All rights reserved under International and Pan-American Copyright Conventions. No part of this book may be reproduced in any manner whatsoever without written permission from the publisher, except in the case of brief quotations embodied in critical articles and reviews.

Publisher: Leah Huete de Maines
Editor: Christen Kincaid
Cover Art and Back Cover Photo: K. Hogan and E.F. Schraeder
Cover Design: Elizabeth Maines McCleavy

Order online: www.finishinglinepress.com
also available on amazon.com

Author inquiries and mail orders:
Finishing Line Press
PO Box 1626
Georgetown, Kentucky 40324
USA

Table of Contents

A Place for Her Thumb 1

This is Not an Elegy 2

Daddy and Other Tragedies of Girlhood 3

Dark Stars 4

Cameras and Ink 5

Under Examination 6

We All Fall 7

Top Ten Rehab 8

YourTunes 9

Junk 10

Another Piece of Her Heart: Untold Stories 11

Sympathetic Characters and Unrelatable Women 12

Click Like Share Laugh Point 13

Villains 14

Performance 15

Flying Trapeze 16

Icons 17

Damaged Women (Turn U On) 18

No Comets at This Time 19

The Notes She Left Behind 20

Ever After 21

Feels 22

Coaxed 23

Jewel Child 24

Twenty-Seven 25

Poems for Amy Winehouse
1983-2011

"Audiences like their blues singers to be miserable."
~ Janis Joplin

A Place for Her Thumb

Something sad in the eyes glows
smooth as the groove of a worry stone

like that hollow hard-edge song she carried
with slung guitar and shadowy voice.

Crowds hung with the hits,
clapping. A chorus of cheering fans

drank the painful good beats,
sank down with demons,

aimed her refrains like sharp arrows,
pointed lyrics like fires and apostrophes

shattering the sting
of her heartbreak strings.

No. No. No
one worried at all.

This Is Not an Elegy
—for Sylvia, Janis, and you

Stay, you listless, voluptuous interloper. A
Jezebel, a never included someone.

She yearned, looking very interested and
jaded, almost nonexistent in sedation.

She's you. Lonely velvet insides and
jailed antagonism. Nailed in, sacrificial.

Smiling. Your laughing voice. Indignant applause
just allows new intrepid songs.

Stolen youth: luscious, violent, inconsolable. Always
joking as now is slipping.

Daddy and Other Tragedies of Girlhood

No one knows the guy. I never knew him,
which is to say, he probably never loved me.

He's maybe not clever enough to imagine.
So he forgot-devoured the women he saw,

swallowed-ignored the feminine in himself.
Parents who don't see

let crushing, inconsistent attention
become an eternal slap. I drifted, unapproved.

He's not present long enough to notice
anything but the bleeding.

He stays distant enough
to reach me only by kick.

Dark Stars

Delight and fortune, celebration whispers a song
of shadow, a meteor-life of corners and recesses.

Heralds of genius include plodding self-destruction
and other fire kisses no one wants to see.

Easy to miss at night, only emerging
like utter dark.

Wallowed and wooed, they infatuate us
weaving a constellation of stories across

a century of nights to swallow one at a time
like burning pills.

Cameras and Ink

Heart in a jar, hey doc, did you examine me?
I'm swimming in vinegar, a brine of declension
choking on last night's dinner.

She checks in, pleas for help
while bloggers laugh and shout,
point cameras and spill ink.

She thrives on decline, they say. Sad drunk!
She apologizes for spectacles.
It's a disease, but not the pretty way

she does it, which is to say,
ashes, ashes we all fall
dead.

Under Examination

Deep breath
        Inhale St. Lucia's salty air

Pulse check
        Exhale negativity

Blood work
        Inhale attention

Rehab
        Exhale doubt

Collapse
        Inhale calm

Intervention
        Exhale gone

We All Fall

color : rainbow :: star : meteor

woman : human :: original : lonely

succeed : fail :: drunk : sober

drug : addict :: ego : anxiety

exploit : aware :: witness : neglect

reward : genius :: ignored : privacy

singer : song :: death : ash

Top Ten Rehab

Enshrined, fame stumbles,
slams on the kitchen floor.
Bleeds tears like needles.

A smokescreen second coming
outlives her.

Tongue dives and all terrible,
a case of something misplaced.

Her sexy hot mess
like any woman
who gets loved too hard.

She's a chorus. A riot of weeping girls,
All apologies.

A slaughterhouse of opinions.
The way Judy Garland is not a sunrise.

YourTunes

Frank as Mercury's short orbit,
one kohl-eyed daddy's girl
launched on a face-booked freeway.

She faded to black as cameras snapped,
clipping and eclipsing
with casual predatory intrusions.

Paparazzi jaws headlined *She's on Crack*,
with pictures of her mouth on a pipe,
memified into a shared a nosedive.

Armed with apps to track favorite celebs,
streaming late-night roams and tearful days
because tabloid targets sell copy.

Like a wild Diana, a lioness who flees
with more than twenty awards
but she only escapes traps one at a time.

So hot at the center of the pyre—
Her apartment now a soft beacon to martyrs,
fame's shrine of cigarettes, booze, and flowers.

Junk

Sleazy delicious men
smiling and scanning skin
for fingerprints.

Broken love like a bruise—
something swollen
and forgotten

sleeps in the melody,
a familiar pinch
or punchline

pulled aside,
asunder.

Her noose, a microphone
swinging.

Another Piece of Her Heart: Untold Stories

Scribbled lyrics. Notebooks full of hearts.
Gossip stronger than schoolgirl crush on acid.

Tabloids' shrinking candles of praise
and shouting winds of blame.

Calculating, dividing strangers
and friends from snowballed awards.

Fury and public condemnation
strong as a preacher's disapproval.

Venting candid, but dishonest. Hints
about the real thing behind the curtain.

Middle of the night, headphones on,
she's a bluebird of fear.

When we're alone with our bottles
mistaking them for friends we can call,

friends who always answer,
the busy business of dream destruction,

like repetition, so much more
lucrative than creation.

Sympathetic Characters and Unrelatable Women

Her fault.
        Hers to lose.

Bad judgment.
        Weak mind.

Pathetic. Loser.
        Irresponsible.

All the loud shades
        of the hysteria rainbow

applied with
        blunt finger paint

smear the rouge of blame
        on her cheeks

so carefully, it took
        two hands to hold her down.

Click Like Share Laugh Point

The public pointed its right-to-know camera
in the face, up the skirt
prodding, *Give us a cheeky smile, love.*

Skinny, coy witch, she knew
what she got herself into
buzzing with all those snarky songs

and deep blues. Breaking
apart is big business, girl. Besides,
an old soul knows her way around.

Notice when the torches light, the villagers
prepare to shake loose the monster
but it's her who comes.

Notice that kid you're booing
isn't a party trick,
how she's not okay.

Villains

No big bad wolf huffed the door down.
Nobody called and nobody came
but the comedians and callouts,
like so many whistles and shivering tambourines.

Back up dancers hopped at the beat,
timed and traced each slow motion replay,
a doctor's x-ray.
This is what unforgiven looks like.

Rewind that— she's playing on pause.
No one sipped the drinks but her
even if someone still poured until it was over,
and we clapped, hoping for a remix.

Performance

Bob Dylan shows up late,
nabs a grand prize

with an effortless impression of cool.
Forget his car salesman ad spots—

the crowds cheer, sing along,
a sea of sways and stomps.

She's staggering now,
suffocating but still posing.

Remember her big voice,
how a catchy tune stitches us together

to witness the dance of her undoing.

Flying Trapeze

How dare she die,
mistake rhymes,

or be bored repeating lines.
How dare she gain weight

or lose weight,
have bad skin

and bad teeth,
bulimia. How dare she

have no shame,
wear that tank top.

How dare she drink so much,
look like that,

be such a bad role model,
roll her eyes, have a temper,

have an affair,
wear that dress,

tattoo herself,
or live so close to death.

Icons

Dim shadows and morning light,
so unforgiving. So honest.

Gray lids, drooping eyes,
a bland chalky film at the lips.

Cigarette dangling from the mouth,
still posing. Strained.

Some-bodies destined
for greatness, stardom.

Some bodies end beneath a sheet.
On stretchers.

A song repeats on the radio. In memorial.
A photoshopped pic appears online.

Not all the music in the world
erases fate.

We'll remember most of her,
wading in her mistakes and music.

Damaged Women (Turn U On)

Bring it on, baby.
All that doe-eyed disappointment
All that hurt indignant rage.

Silky songs full of vulgar needs.
Bring your ego and insecurity,
panic and fury. Sing where it hurts.

Sing us how you fall apart.
Give us adorable songs,
we'll cheer along. Fix it.

Or feed it.
Fuck it.
Sell it.

No Comets at This Time

Audiences hunger for that blood-juice headline,
chase down nasty tongued demon-lovers
who swat photographers like flies.

To gnaw and gnash on the brittle bones of wispy drunks.
To lick up scattered dreams, weep with grieving parents.
To crave those swollen salty reward-tears!

Candles light. The mourners
gather in song, their arms raised.
Bright sparks glow like cigarette ends.

A public tomb at your door,
an ashtray of regrets. Anything
to burn away what lands in dirt.

The Notes She Left Behind

Microphone thin, a bony thing
unfeathered to the skin,
fleeting and coarse.

A melody subs for
where the heartache went.

Who knows what kept her so taut,
looming over two notes
like a town drunk walking a line.

Doubt slides into a hiding place
where songs live.

Get back on stage and sing.
Nobody wants to see that.
That girl needs to filter herself.

Exceptions and rules are like women.
It's not so hard to like women,
but that kind of woman is impossible.

Ever After

Glitter dares
big talent.
Magic lights

big risks.
Tickets sell
big deals.
Records break

big hits.
Lines blur
big costs.

Fairy tales
so often
end badly.

Feels

Smoky voiced sirens
distant and detached
too many injuries
for bandages
so the songs
release demons.

Let's tape over the spots
too ugly to look at.
Swoon and dance, croon
and kick back a few
while she spikes joy
with something to pity.

Coaxed

Hum along with the verse,
each new release an
incantation that beguiles.

Crowds chant her name,
expect greatness, but
it's just some skinny sad girl

singing from her veins
about the awe of loneliness,
wanting a ribbon of love for her hair,

still finding blank eyes,
gaps where trust should go.
Tears like evidence.

That's the thing about
giving up on life—
it's catchy.

Jewel Child

Rhythm guitar and a slipknot life
girl you were magic at the core,

with a head full of golden dreams
and thorny roses.

Remember that time you sang
and the world lit up like a diamond?

Remember how your onyx eyes
and pearl of a voice crashed cars?

You'd turn heartbreak upside down
into a rain of harmonies,

Showing up late, you turned addiction
into a lesson nobody wanted to learn.

Twenty-Seven

Pause once.
Remember the intersections
however brief or long ago

when snap judgments tilted our directions,
attractions collided with bad sex,
odd ends upended plans,

and adulthood criss-crossed childish dreams.
Recall that unmet yen for nostalgia, friends,
all the things we could have yet become.

Still too young, really, for a lot of things
we did, but the body recovered well then.
A generational wall builds itself

around that time. We're not yet thirty.
Before that happens, we'll list
the million things we want to do next.

The people we'll meet,
the ones we'll forget,
and the ones we'll become.

Knowing what we cherish most will fade,
a background singer's homage
to our unmade plans.

Don't worry about much
or over commit,
we tell ourselves:

we have time.
And we do
until we don't.

An active member in the Horror Writers Association, **E.F. Schraeder** is the author of *Liar: Memoir of a Haunting* (Omnium Gatherum, 2021), the story collection *Ghastly Tales of Gaiety and Greed* (Omnium Gatherum, 2020), and two poetry chapbooks. Recent work has appeared in *Lost Contact, Mobius: The Journal of Social Change, Lavender Review*, and other journals and anthologies. Schraeder's nonfiction has appeared in *Vastarien: A Literary Journal; Radical Teacher; the American Library Association's Intellectual Freedom blog*, and elsewhere. Awarded first place in Crystal Lake Publishing's 2021 Poetry Contest, Schraeder is a former philosophy professor who holds an interdisciplinary Ph.D. and advanced degree in Library Science. E. F. Schraeder believes in ghosts, magic, and dogs.

www.ingramcontent.com/pod-product-compliance
Lightning Source LLC
Chambersburg PA
CBHW022127090426
42743CB00008B/1040